Milarepa
Tibet's Greatest Meditator

Introducing Meditation

For Beginners to More Experienced

Introducing Meditation

For Beginners To More Experienced

Ven. Gelong Karma Jiga

Edited by

Helen Macrae and Dr Julie Wardrop (Ani Lamdron)

NALJORPA PUBLISHING

NALJORPA PUBLISHING
51 Reform Street
Dundee, Scotland, UK. DD1 1SL
Tel. 01382 872020
info@dundee.rokpa.org

Printed by AK2 Pro Pvt. Limited Printers
No 25 Battaramulla Road, Etul Kotte, Sri Lanka.

British Library Cataloguing in Publication Data.
A catalogue record for this book is available from the British Library

ISBN13   978-1-906119-00-3

This book has been written at the request of Karma Jiga's students.
All proceeds from this book are donated to the Rokpa Trust, which is dedicated to improving the lives of others. The Trust was founded by Dr Akong Tulku Rinpoche, a Tibetan Buddhist meditation master who is also the co-founder of Samye Ling Monastery and Tibetan Centre which nestles in the southern border hills of Scotland.

Further Resources

A guided recorded session is available from the Rokpa Dundee online shop to help you establish your habit to practise. www.dundee.rokpa.org/shop

Ven. Karma Jiga's Centres

Rokpa Dundee	**Rokpa Highlands**	**Rokpa Aberdeen**
www.dundee.rokpa.org	www.highlands.rokpa.org	www.aberdeen.rokpa.org

This book is dedicated to
His Holiness the 17th Gyalwa Karmapa,
The 12th Tai Situpa,
The 18th Doolmo Chöje Rinpoche
Chöje Akong Tulku Rinpoche
&
Lama Yeshe Losal Rinpoche
without whom
nothing would be possible.

Contents

Foreword

MEDITATION is becoming very popular in the West now, particularly among people living lives that they find extremely stressful. There are numerous self-help books and many people who have built entire careers out of the distress of others. And, because of our wish in the Western World to intellectualise various aspects of our lives, and to intellectualise about our minds in particular, much of the advice and therapy on offer is often complex and very often ineffective as a result. Rather than helping, it compounds our already complicated thought processes. But it need not be so.

Here, we cut through all the complexities and offer you effective, easy to use techniques which have been tried and tested over many centuries. These methods gleaned from the Tibetan Buddhist tradition have stood the test of time and have been proved to work, even in our fast-paced 21st century lives.

The methods and the advice are brought to you by the Venerable Gelong Karma Jiga, a Westerner, educated in Britain but who, having spent the past thirty years under the direct guidance of senior Tibetan Buddhist Masters, has been able to meld Eastern and Western philosophies to create a unique understanding of just what we in the West need to do in order to help ourselves and change our lives for the better. Changing our lives for the better not only benefits us, but also those around us. This book should be useful for beginners and those with some knowledge wishing to further their Practice.

Helen Macrae, Rokpa Highlands, 2007

1. Meditation

The Tibetan word for focusing the mind, SAMTEN, implies taking control of your mental processes to remove confusion and suffering. This lessens the disturbances in your mind, which will eventually lead to a peaceful state of mind and more happiness. In this book you will be introduced to the primary meditation practice of SHINAY, which conveys the meaning of peace or pacification.

Shinay is a Tibetan word. The first syllable Shi or 'peace' implies that, the presence of thoughts and the movement of thoughts don't disturb your mind. Shi also refers to the principle of the gradual pacification or settling of these thoughts through the repeated application of your chosen practice method. The second syllable, nay, refers to the stability or reduction in the amount of thinking and your involvement with thinking. This arises through the focussed mind resting in attention or absorption on whatever you've chosen to use as the focus for your practice, for example your breath.

So the word Shinay refers to both the process of meditation and the result of the process of the first or primary stage in meditation. Initially you need to understand that meditation is working with your mind, and that in order to meditate, you should look into your mind. To do this you need to know what meditation is in the first place. There are two distinct stages. The first is to reduce the intensity and volume of thought in your mind and the second is to realise the nature of whatever thoughts arise in your mind, and finally, gain insight into what mind itself is. In this book, we are dealing with the first stage, how to reduce the intensity and volume of thinking which arises in your mind.

Next, we need to know what causes us to think so much. The cause is, that we pay attention to all the thoughts which arise in our mind and attach a great deal of importance to them, that's our habit – a very old habit! This keeps our mind thinking. So, it stands to reason that we need to stop paying attention to the thoughts and learn to pay attention to something other than the thinking. We learn to do that by repeating this process over and over again until we just rest the mind without thinking, whenever we want to.

So Why Should We Meditate?

"The practice of meditation in spiritual development is one of gaining greater freedom of mind and control over our own experience". Kalu Rinpoche, 20th century Tibetan Buddhist master.

Many Buddhist meditation texts explain why we should meditate. For example: to tame the mind and find inner peace, to discover what is real and what is unreal, to discover the nature of reality, to improve mental stability, to recognise the true nature of mind – these are just some of the reasons given. In the beginning however, it is more likely that we are trying to learn to relax, reduce stress, tension, anxiety and the frustrations of everyday life or as another great Tibetan master, Dilgo Khyentse Rinpoche said " to make the best of a bad job!"

What's the best way to go about meditating?

First of all, where we meditate is important. If you're a beginner, find a quiet place, with few people around, where there's not much talking or laughter. You will be less easily distracted in a place like this. It's been your habit to pay attention to everything around you, so this will make meditation easier. Most of us feel more relaxed and comfortable in natural surroundings, around pure natural sounds like running water, the sound of the ocean, the wind in the trees, birds singing and so on. That's why, in times gone by, meditators and masters sought out, and stayed in such places.

These meditators found that sitting outside in the countryside and other quiet places helps their mind relax. Places in the mountains, hilltops, by a calm sea or lake are particularly good places. They offer plenty of space, with natural sounds and little to distract you. Failing that you should try to find the quietest place possible. For us, with our busy modern lifestyles, that's more likely to be indoors.

If you meditate indoors, your room should be uncluttered, to prevent distractions. It should be clean, tidy and with air flowing through it. It shouldn't be too hot or too cold. Too hot and you could end up feeling sleepy and dull, too cold you won't be able to settle. It's better to keep the room a little cool, as this helps to keep your mind clear.

What Next?

Once you've found the best place and conditions for your practice, it's important to prepare for the session by wearing loose fitting clothes. It's also very important to learn how to sit properly. You should sit according to your physical condition, and not try to force your body into positions which cause pain and difficulty as you won't be able to meditate and even want to stop your meditation session.

2. Posture

The Types Of Posture

It's best to sit in a cross-legged posture if you can manage. The lotus or Vajra posture, as it is known in Tibetan Buddhism, and the half-lotus postures are best. Once you become skilled in sitting like this, you'll be able to sit for long periods with the spine erect, which keeps the energies flowing proerly in the body. If you can't manage this, then don't struggle or cause yourself pain by trying to sit in this way in the beginning, simply sit cross-legged, which most of us can manage easily. If you can't manage those, then just sit in a chair. You might have to develop your posture gradually, going through a series of different positions until reaching the ideal sitting position. The main thing is to avoid forcing the posture. You'll be less likely to want to meditate if you cause yourself pain.

The Lotus And Half-Lotus Postures

For the lotus or half-lotus position, fold the left leg inside first, the heel pointing towards the base of the spine. The right leg is drawn in with the sole upwards resting on the thigh of the left leg. To sit in the full lotus posture, put your left foot and ankle up on the right thigh and then put the right foot and ankle up on the left thigh.

If you are not used to sitting is these positions, you should gradually and gently train your body, allowing it to adapt to the posture. Forcing your body into these positions could create problems, so gently and gradually build up the length of time you sit in these positions.

How to Use Your Cushion

The first thing to understand is that the cushion is not really used to sit on! Ideally it's placed under the base of the spine to help straighten the spine and keep it erect. You'll have to experiment to find the most comfortable position in the beginning. As your body adapts to the posture, you'll have to use different sizes of cushions. If you are used to the cross legged posture, then a small, square, hard cushion two to four inches thick is normally used, but this all depends on what you find comfortable. You may have to use a higher cushion.

If you find crossing one or both legs uncomfortable, then sit with your legs loosely crossed. You can also kneel, using a low meditation stool, sitting in the Burmese posture, with the legs tucked under the stool. Others kneel and place a cushion between their backside and calves. For some, it's best to sit in a chair. It really depends on what you find most comfortable and what suits you physically.

Straightening The Spine

You should stretch and straighten your spine, holding it as erect as you can in a relaxed way. Your spine connects your central nervous system to all the major organs in your body. If your spine is not held properly, it can cause pain or discom¬fort in different parts of your body. According to the Buddhist tradition we also have energy channels running throughout the body. Holding the spine straight and erect straightens our energy channels and also allows the energies to flow freely through the body. While sitting, your body should feel relaxed and balanced; your shoulders should be straight and relaxed. The key to proper posture is to have a straight spine and a relaxed body.

The Positioning Of The Hands

There are two positions for the hands, resting the hands palms down on the knees with the elbows straightened, known as the lion posture in some texts or, alterna¬tively, resting the open right hand on top of the open left hand with the thumbs lightly touching, one and a half inches below the navel. This is called the Dhyani Mudra. The hands shouldn't be held too high, too low or have the thumbs pressed together, they should be touching gently.

The Positioning Of The Neck

Your head should be very slightly inclined, with the chin tucked slightly inwards and the neck pulled very slightly back. There's a slight sensation felt at the Adam's apple, it's not like pressure, just a slight feeling, more like a sensation.

The Positioning Of The Mouth And Jaw

Your jaw should be relaxed, lips gently touching, teeth slightly open, with the tip of the tongue touching the roof of the mouth and the back of the top teeth.

The Eyes

Your eyes should be slightly open, gazing downwards, one to two metres in front. You should relax the focus of your eyes and hold your gaze in a gentle manner.

Posture In General

If you make a conscious effort to go through each point of the posture when you begin your meditation session, you'll soon get used to it and it will become second nature. There are two main points to the posture: straighten the spine and relax the body. You should not feel any pain when sitting in the meditation posture. If you find it difficult to sit like this, or there's too much tension in the posture, relax your body, relax the posture. It's okay to support your knees with cushions if you need to prevent discomfort. You have to find the way to sit that suits your body best. You have to learn to relax into the posture. One analogy used, is to consider how cotton wool is put together. It's very loose and relaxed. While all the fibres are separate, at the same time they hold together, but in a loose way. Our posture should be balanced in the same way, not too loose and not too tight. Sitting like this helps your mind feel more awake, more alert.

A More Detailed Explanation of the Posture

The explanations given by the Buddha in sutras, of The Seven Points of the Meditation Posture, or The Seven Dharmas of Vairochana, are instructions on how to sit during mediation practice. The term Dharma has many meanings, but in this context refers to the activity of taking up the posture of Vairochana. Vairochana is a Sanskrit word which was translated as namthang in Tibetan. Namthang means, to have mental clarity and awareness. So, the very act of taking up this posture sharpens the mind, and brings about mental clarity. It was discovered that this was the best way to hold your body to develop the ability to focus the mind and to develop its ability to rest in attention.

The Vajrayana or Tantric Teachings

Cultivating this ability to sit well, comfortably, in a relaxed way, will eventually enable your mind to rest in an effortless non-conceptual experience of bliss and clarity. According to the Buddha's Vajrayana teachings, the mind and the energy 'winds' that move throughout the body are inseparably linked. When the energy winds flow properly the mind will be focused; when they are not flowing properly the mind won't be focused. These winds run through energy channels within our body. There are three main channels. They're called the central channel, the left channel and the right channel.

In our present situation, the winds normally pass through the right and left channels. They act as the vehicle for our deluded thoughts. These delusions stop when the energy winds are directed into the central channel. So the eventual purpose of the meditation is to direct these winds into the central channel and end the delusion.

When you hold your body with the spine straight, the channels are straight and positioned correctly. The winds then flow more freely through the channels helping the mind to relax and focus. That's why the seven-point posture is so important. Simply assuming the individual positions of the posture correctly brings about a sense of tranquillity and openness in your mind.

The posture in relation to the emotions and energy winds which flow through the body:

The Legs:
Sitting in the Vajra posture or cross legged controls the downward energy and acts as a remedy for jealousy.

The Back or Spine:
Straightening the spine like a spear or like a row of coins, one on top of the other, will place the energy wind of the space/earth element in the central channel and acts as a remedy for ignorance.

The Hands:
Placing the hands in the Dhyani Mudra, holding them below the navel and pulling the shoulders back like a vulture's wings encourages the wind of the water element into the central channel and acts as a remedy for anger and aggression

The Head and Neck:
Keeping the neck bent like a hook induces the wind of the fire element into the central channel and acts as a remedy for desire/attachment.

The Eyes, Mouth, Lips And Teeth
Having the eyes neither wide open nor tight shut, but relaxing the focus and gazing at a point four finger widths from the tip of the nose, draws the wind of the air element into the central channel and also acts as a remedy for pride, as is placing the jaw, the lips, the teeth and the tongue correctly.

According to the classification of the energy winds in the text called the Six Yoga's of Naropa there are 5 major winds.

1. The downward going wind controlling the discard and retention of waste.
2. The upward going wind controlling swallowing, speaking and other activities of the throat.
3. The life sustaining wind maintaining the spark of life.
4. The equalising wind which covers the functions of digestion and the separation of wastes.
5. The all pervading wind which deals with all the motor activities or movement within the body.

As you can see from the above the winds can be classified in different ways. They are combined in the table below

The Importance Of Proper Posture

The table shows how each part of the posture affects the energy movements in our body, how it affects our body's functions, how the posture is related to the elements within the body and how it relates to our emotional states.

WIND	FUNCTION	ELEMENT	Position of Posture	REMEDY FOR
Downward	Bowel Control	Earth	Legs and Spine	Jealousy
Upward	Throat	Air	Eyes, Mouth, Lips and Teeth	Pride
Life Sustaining	Breathe Consciousness	Space	Spine and Shoulders	Ignorance
Equalising	Digestion Separation Of Waste	Fire	Neck and Throat	Desire Attachmen
All Pervading	Motor Movements, Muscle, Circulation Etc	Water	Hands	Anger Aggression

It should now be clear that how you hold your body affects how you feel – not only in your meditation but also in your daily life. This can be proved very simply. Just straighten your spine and relax your body, you can feel the difference immediately.

Why is this? It's because your body and mind are intimately linked. What you do with your body affects your mind. It also follows that if your mind is not relaxed, then your body won't be relaxed. Those who experience stress know what this feels like.

So, What Happens If You Don't Sit Properly?

Sitting badly blocks the energy flow in the channels and produces imbalance in your mind. It can change your feelings and emotions. You may feel good to begin with, but sitting awkwardly can cause physical and mental problems. You could suffer emotional disturbance during the meditation sessions and after the meditation sessions in your daily life. This affects your own behaviour and can affect how you behave towards others.

The Difficulties Arising From The Legs

Bad positioning of the legs can cause your legs to "go to sleep," or to develop "pins & needles" to restrict, block or stop the blood flow. The same applies to the energy channels.

The Difficulties Arising From The Eyes

Meditating while staring upwards can cause a feeling of lightness, comfort and an experience of clarity to begin with. But later, this can give rise sensations of floating or speediness, which can transform into feelings of anger and frustration.

The Difficulties Arising From Slouching

Slouching or slumping brings about a feeling of comfort and relaxation. If you continue like this, you're mind will become more slothful and you'll tend to fall asleep, which increases your ignorance.

The Difficulties Caused By not sitting straight

If you lean to the right while meditating, you'll eventually generate more pleasurable thoughts than usual. You'll tend to follow these thoughts because you like them, and eventually end up being distracted by them. Leaning to the left while meditating, will eventually generate more unpleasant thoughts and desires than usual. You'll tend to pay attention to and follow those thoughts too.

You might find it difficult and uncomfortable to hold your body in the proper posture when you first begin to meditate. You may suffer a little, and experience some discomfort. However, if you practice going through the stages of the posture every session, and hold the posture for short periods, relaxing and then taking up the posture again, repeating this many times you'll experience the benefits of sitting properly and eventually both your body and mind will relax into the posture, and your mind will become more stable.

3. The Practice

The Buddha said in the sutras, "The essence of the dharma is taming the mind. In a quiet, solitary place, on a comfortable meditation cushion, sit in the proper meditation posture, your back erect, maintaining the correct position of the body, and engage in the practice of Samadhi" – which is resting your mind in attention itself.

The Outer Conditions for Successful Meditation

Here again, we'll highlight that it's good to meditate in a quiet, flat and level place and that you'll need a meditation mat and cushion. The mat keeps your legs and ankles from hurting. The cushion helps you maintain good posture. The texts mention that the cushion should be three to four fingers' width deep. Now you've fulfilled the outer conditions for your meditation practice to be successful.

The Inner Conditions for Successful Meditation

Next we look at how to reduce the volume and intensity of our thoughts. Normally we use words like peace, tranquillity and stillness. To bring about this stillness or peace means you have to know how to help your mind to think less. To do this you have to pay less attention to your thoughts. In fact you have to learn to pay attention to something else! But your old habit of paying attention to your thoughts still persists. So, your meditation session consists of moving between paying attention to your thoughts and paying attention and resting the attention on something other than your thoughts – your breath, for example. You move from old habit to new habit, back and forth, back and forth. That's your meditation session in a nutshell. At least that's it in the beginning.

However, if you commit yourself to cultivating this new skill, then you'll find that the time you spend paying attention to your thoughts will lessen, and, eventually, you will think less and your mind will relax. If you repeat this regularly, for short periods, your mind will become used to this. As your mind becomes used to it, you can gradually extend the length of time you do this. As you continue, your mind will become more relaxed and less agitated, your body will be more relaxed and your life will begin to change. You'll be able to relax into your life.

Taking Things Further

If you take this further, learning to focus, to pay attention, and to rest in the attention, then the strength of your old habit will lessen. Not only that, if you realise how this works, you can apply it to everything you do in your life. It becomes meditation in action. It's important you understand this. Having understood this, you can apply and use this in your busy life, throughout your day, anywhere, any time, if you really want to. That's why it's so relevant today, right now. If you don't understand this, then you've missed the point of why you should meditate! We have to carry the process into our daily lives; otherwise, we'll just carry on in the same old way, doing the same old things, creating the same old problems and difficulties for ourselves.

Understanding What Happens

In the beginning, when you sit down and meditate, you'll see that you think, in fact, that you think a lot! At this point many of us decide to stop meditating, because we feel that we're not meditating. It appears that all we do is think, think endlessly! We give up at this point because we haven't understood that it's our habit to think. We've been do-ing it for a long, long time. So it's not really surprising that all we seem to do is think. We're developing a new habit, paying attention to something other than our thinking and that takes time!

If you continue, and look at what you think about, you'll see that you think about the past and you think about the future; you'll think about what you should be doing; think about what you should have done, you'll remember things, things you forgot, things you did; you'll write the shopping list, think of the family, about your job, about your holiday... endless things. If you follow these thoughts, you'll continue with your old habit, you'll continue to pay attention to the thoughts or whatever else arises in your mind. That's not meditation, that's thinking!

In order to help you reduce the volume and intensity of your thinking you have to remind yourself to pay attention to something else, your breath for example. You have to realise that your habit of paying attention to your thoughts is very strong and you'll forget to pay attention to your breath or whatever you've chosen to focus on. Knowing this, experiencing this, you'll have to keep reminding yourself, reminding yourself to remember to pay attention to the breath, for example!

You have to try to stay alert, and be aware of what your mind is doing. This is how you know when to remind your mind to pay attention to something 'other than the think-ing'. It's like a fire, if you keep adding fuel to it, the fire will continue to burn. If you stop feeding it with fuel, the flames will die down and eventually the fire will go out. Your mind is like this. If you want to think less, to have a less busy mind, a more clear

12

and stable mind, then you have to cultivate and encourage this ability to rest the mind on something other than the thoughts and reduce your involvement with the thoughts, feelings and emotions. This process is called developing mindfulness and awareness.

Continuity

To develop this new and positive habit requires effort and application. Not only that, it requires continuity of effort and application. You have to repeat the process over and over again. Repetition involves setting aside the same time every day to do this. It also relates to how you apply your mind when you meditate. This is how you developed your old bad habits, and this is how you're going to cultivate the new and useful, beneficial habits. If you don't understand why you meditate and why you should apply yourself, then your practice won't be of benefit to you. Not only that, you'll just strengthen your involvement with your thoughts and external things, causing you to become totally carried away by your thoughts, and you'll continue as before, constantly stimulated by your thoughts and emotional patterns.

So, developing inner stillness or quiet requires that you become less involved with these distractions. It requires making a commitment within, to find the time to develop your ability to focus, to focus on whatever you've chosen to use for the practice, and cultivating your ability to become less distracted by events of the past or the possibilities for the future; by external and internal events. It requires maintaining your awareness and your ability to focus and finally resting in attention. It also entails bringing the attention back, when you realise it has wandered or become involved with thoughts.

How To Meditate

Now, having some understanding of the outer and inner conditions for the practice, you should develop your ability to meditate. Having sat in the posture and chosen what you would like to use for the meditation, you should focus your mind on this. Normally, you might say concentrate. But, in the west, the word concentrate implies shutting things out, excluding or trying to stop external or internal things interfering with your concentration. When applied to meditation we're not trying to stop thoughts or anything else interfering, we're 'placing' our focus to allow our mind to settle, to settle naturally, of its own accord with little or no effort.

So, How To Do This?

First, choose a method that you like or an object you find pleasing. Direct your attention to this object, then focus your mind, hold your attention and finally relax into the attention, just barely paying attention, applying just enough effort to maintain your attention, finally, becoming absorbed in the attention. Remember that you're not trying to shut things out, but rather, focus in a relaxed way, acknowledging and accepting all the external and internal noise without becoming involved with it. So, to clarify this

13

process, focus and then relax into the focusing. If you try to focus too strongly your mind will become agitated. If applied too lightly, your mind might wander. You need to practise this, to become familiar with it, to perfect and maintain it, and eventually to be able to do this at will. Placing your mind and holding the attention is a bit like watching a feather fall and then feeling what it would be like for it to land on something, and maintaining that feeling in a very relaxed way.

4. Approaching The Meditation Session

Attitude

You should approach the session with a positive frame of mind. Remind yourself that your meditation will help to relax your mind, generate more stability and clarity, which will allow you to live your daily life in a more relaxed and open way. Remind yourself of this before the session.

Effort

Nothing is obtained without effort. In order to develop a calm and stable mind, continuity of commitment is essential. You should set aside time in the morning and evening to meditate. Twenty to thirty minutes a session would help prepare you for the day and relieve stress at the end of it. If you're a beginner then divide this time into short sessions without leaving the meditation cushion. Apply yourself for a few minutes and then relax again, repeating this a number of times throughout the session.

Posture

Sitting in the correct posture as we have now discovered, is very important. You should choose how you sit according to your body's capabilities, gradually training your body to sit in the seven-point posture or the best that you can manage according to your physical condition. Now that you know, and have felt the benefits of sitting properly during your meditation session, it would be a good idea to remind yourself of this during the day. Sit properly for a few minutes, stretching the spine and sitting up straight every now and then for a minute or two throughout your day.

Preparation

Relax your body and mind, using whichever method you find suitable. If you are a Buddhist, then recite prayers that you find inspiring before beginning your meditation session.

What to Use for Your Meditation Practice

The practice can be done in many different ways using both internal and external objects, which can be real or imagined: with form, or without form. Some of these are listed below.

External Examples:

These can be pure or impure, large or small.

Impure, large - this could be the sky, a tree, a wall or pillar.

Impure, small - this could be a candle flame, pebble or piece of wood.

Pure - focus on a small Buddha statue or imagine one.

Internal Examples:

Impure - imagine a sphere of white light between the eyes

Pure - imagine a smiling Buddha on an eight-petalled lotus in your heart.

Using The Breath

Focus on the sensations at the diaphragm as you breathe in and out.
Focus on the sensations at the tip of the nose as you breathe in and out.
Focus on counting the breath, in and out, up to twenty-one.

There are many different methods. Only a few are listed here.

5. Overcoming Obstacles

In addition to using the correct posture and techniques when meditating, you also need guidelines and methods to overcome the difficulties and obstacles which arise when you practise meditation. The two main obstacles encountered during your meditation are: mental dullness and agitation.

The Causes Of Mental Dullness

Mental dullness or drowsiness can be caused by: meditating in a dark room; by hot, humid, close or heavy weather conditions. It may also be caused by trying to meditate after eating too much or could be the result of meditating after physical exertion. You might find it difficult to sustain the posture or focus effectively if you try to meditate under these conditions. When mental dullness arises, you may not be sure of what's happening, or, even if there's anything happening at all! When your mind is in this state it can feel dull, heavy, drowsy or even sleepy, which means you're not really meditating at all. There's no real clarity or alertness in your mind. When these difficulties or obstacles arise you have to counteract and overcome them, you have to apply antidotes.

Antidotes for mental dullness

There are several things you can do to help. Here are a few suggestions:

You can forcefully raise your body up and sit very straight.
You can change how you hold your head and your eyes.
Raise your head and eyes and look upwards.
If it is a warm day, sit in a cool breeze or keep all the windows to your room open.
Keep a bright light to the front and above you.

Visualise a bright light in the middle of your brow, a dot, the size of a pea, white, clear, lustrous, spherical and extremely clear, then direct your mind towards it.

When you exhale, visualise your breath as a very brilliant flow of light going up. When you inhale, visualise the brilliant light coming in and lighting up your whole inside like a lamp being lit up.

Splash your face with running cold water.
Keep a wet cloth beside you and wipe your face with it occasionally.
Run cold water over the backs of your heels, a trick used by Christian nuns.
Place your feet in cold water.
Eat light food to promote a feeling of lightness in the mind.

If you apply these methods, your mind will become more awake and alert, and gradually return to its normal state. At that point restart your practice in the normal way. Don't use these methods as your regular practice; only use them when you need to.

Antidotes For Agitation

There are two types of agitation, mental agitation and physical agitation. There are different causes and remedies for each of these two.

The Causes Of Mental Agitation

The second most common problem arising during meditation is agitation or restlessness. You become over excited and your mind won't stay where you want to place it. Even if you manage to place and rest your mind on the breath, for example, it starts to wander. This can be brought about by a number of things, like: having an argument, physical exertion, feeling anxious, angry or resentful before the session, all of these will agitate your mind. Even if you manage to sit properly, you could find that you're distracted, agitated or tense and that your mind won't settle during the session.

To Eliminate Mental Agitation

When your mind is agitated, relax your body from the normal erect meditation position. Loosen up your whole body structure; gradually relax the spine and the muscles throughout your body so that your whole body is very relaxed and at ease. Close your eyes. Now imagine a black dot at your seat, this makes your mind more subdued and bends the mind downwards. As you feel more grounded and the mind settles, raise your body up gradually, gently and slowly, and begin to assume the meditation posture positions again. When your mind is well settled begin to follow the breath in the normal way.

Physical Agitation

If your body becomes restless, fidgety, and you can't sit still, you should practise walking meditation to use this excess energy in a helpful way. This means focusing on the breaths while walking, for example, which also helps reduce mental agitation. If this worsens and you suffer from strong agitation during your sessions, you should eat a heavy fatty diet to restore balance to the winds, which will make the mind less agitated.

Meditating Intelligently

To meditate properly, tranquillity, stability, openness and a degree of clarity of mind are required. If you have difficulties, intensifying your efforts could make the situation worse, causing physical problems, stress and headaches. Continuing your practice without applying remedies could cause even more disturbance and frustration, which is the opposite of meditation practice. To maintain a balanced approach to your meditation you have to try to develop constant awareness and apply intelligence to the situations that arise as you practise. This helps maintain the quality and continuity of your meditation.

The Benefits And Results Of Meditation

Developing tranquillity, stability and clarity of mind helps in daily life. It improves how you relate to yourself and others. It enables you to develop your dharma practice, to develop your positive side and reduce your negative side. It's not about going to war with your mind or sensational events in your mind or instant dramatic changes to your life. The results and nature of the practice are very simple, clear and straightforward. You'll gain benefit from the very beginning. Through continuing your meditation you'll recognise the changes that take place in your mind. The more you meditate the more you benefit. You'll see the results for yourself, without needing to have them confirmed by others.

6. The Levels Of Practice

You'll discover that you have many kinds of thoughts and that many things will distract you. There'll be conflict between trying to focus and follow the breath and being distracted by thoughts and external things. When this happens you might feel that you're not meditating properly or even that there's little or no benefit from the practice. There's also the possibility that when you're not meditating there appears to be less thoughts and distractions than when you were meditating. It's at this point you may want to stop the practice, because you feel all you do is think, not meditate. What's actually happening during the session is that you're becoming more aware of what's going on in your mind. You're actually seeing yourself think! This is a good sign; it means you're becoming more aware. You should keep practicing, observe the changes, and see your mind gradually change, gradually become more calm and relaxed.

Distraction

Most of the time we're distracted by many kinds of coarse and subtle thoughts. Your thoughts are stimulated by your senses, which are continually making contact with the world around you. These thoughts and distractions are your main focus, the things you pay attention to most. The stream of thoughts seems endless. There's no gap in the thinking to allow you to see the volume and intensity of these distracting thoughts. Meditation, however, helps us to pay attention to and focus on one thing: the breath for example, or whatever you have chosen for your practice. Through trying to meditate, you'll see clearly how distracted you are and what's really happening in your mind. It will allow you to see the amount of thinking we do, how intense it is. If it's like this during a meditation session, then what must it be like the rest of the time?

Focus

It is only when we begin to channel and focus our attention that we can see the flow of thoughts. It's like channelling the water leaving a lake, channelling it through a pipe. Then we can see the power, and become aware of the quantity of the water as it leaves the lake. It's not that there's more water in the lake, its just being confined or contained as a river is when it flows through a gorge. So these initial experiences in our meditation are the first signs that the meditation is working. We are seeing clearly what's actually going on for the first time. There's no need to feel discouraged or disappointed, you should be happy at seeing what is actually happening and continue to practice.

The Waterfall, the River and the Ocean

This intense activity in your mind is compared to a waterfall. It's like water continuously pouring over a cliff. It's the first stage, the first discovery, in your meditation practice. Once again, it is now that many people give up. They say, "I'm only thinking, that's all I seem to do, the meditation isn't working". They give up at this point because they haven't understood this first stage of the practice. So, there's no need to become annoyed or disappointed, or think that you've failed, or it's no use, it's not working. Simply continue your practice.

As you continue to meditate, you will begin to notice a change. Thoughts will come and go and you'll still be distracted, but there will be fewer thoughts, not so much thinking, and you'll be less likely to follow the thoughts. Your wish to follow them will begin to lose its power and you'll be able to return to the breath more easily. This is the sign that the basic meditation is going well.

Your meditation experience will vary, from following the thoughts, to being able to focus as you practice. It will keep changing. This is known as the river, the second stage in the development of your practice. It's like a river, meandering through a wide valley, the flow is not so concentrated, the water runs smoothly. When the river twists and turns or the water runs over rocks or uneven ground the water is stimulated, there's an interruption to the flow, the water bubbles up or there's turbulence. It's the same with your mind, sometimes it will be agitated, and sometimes you'll follow the thoughts. In the same way, just as a river sometimes flows calmly and smoothly without any disturbance, you'll be able to follow the breath for a short time without distraction. At this point, you may be distracted occasionally, but you won't be overwhelmed by your distraction. You'll be able to return more easily to a calm and peaceful state of mind, while you remain focused on the breath.

In the third stage, even more change will take place. You will be able to maintain your awareness and follow the breath almost all of the time. However, every now and then there will be some distractions. This stage is known as, the ocean without waves. At this point, your mind and your practice are beginning to stabilise. You feel more confident and you'll begin to trust in what you're doing. Most of the time the ocean is calm, but now and again a wave appears in this ocean. The disturbance on the surface caused by this wave gradually and gently settles back down, into the ocean itself.

24

At this point you experience some distraction while most of the time you can rest and relax into the attention as your mind becomes more stable and clear.

Through continuing your meditation, you will experience the fourth stage of your Shinay Practice. It's called, like the calm ocean without wind. At this stage, you can now sit and meditate for as long as you want, with no distraction. Although subtle thoughts arise now and then, they don't interfere with the basic technique of following the breath, which means your new habit has overcome the old habit of following the thoughts and you can now rest and relax your mind on the breath for as long as you want.

To reach this level of practice you will have to apply yourself to the practice constantly, repeatedly and conscientiously over a long period of time. Before reaching this level of practice, you will have had to go through each of the stages, one by one. At this point your practice is stable. You can rest your mind at will and have complete power and control over the practice, while experiencing an open and peaceful mind state. In turn the power and intensity of your negative emotions is reduced. As a result, you'll become more considerate, gentle, and patient. You'll have more energy, be less confused and relate to things more clearly, which is very rewarding and very beneficial.

Due to your practice, you'll be less likely to react negatively and be able to deal with frustration and anger internally, in your mind, without the need to react outwardly. This is a long way from when you first began to meditate, where you discovered how disturbed and worried you were, discovered how you tried to suppress and control your emotions and found out just how restless a mind you had.

When your mind becomes calm, clear and stable through your Shinay practice, you feel joy and happiness. You'll feel warmth towards others, become more tolerant and kind, enjoying your life more, through living in a more balanced and less confused way. Those are the potential benefits of your efforts, and those benefits will extend into your daily life, helping you and those around you. These stages can also be presented as nine levels related to your ability to focus, pay attention and rest in the attention as outlined in the table below. There are other ways of presenting these stages but this will do for now.

The Nine Levels Of Stabilising The Mind

1 Placing the mind	Focus on object for short time
2 Focusing for longer	Focusing for longer on object
3 Placing after distraction	Returning to focus after distraction
4 Continuously restoring the focus	Repeatedly returning to focus
5 Establishing control	Joyful, relaxed & enthusiastic practice
6 Establishing peace	Only occasional wandering
7 Complete peace	Through placing awareness on any thought
8 Resting continuously	Very little effort required to focus
9 Resting naturally	Can place and rest the mind at will

Some Very Important Advice

You should study under the guidance of a qualified teacher from a lineage that you can trace, and have confidence in. The practices outlined here involves working with your mind, which is very fragile indeed, as you can see from your own mood changes. Being aware of this, it's best to work with someone experienced in these practices, someone whom you feel you can relate to and through this develop confidence in your ability and their experience by applying yourself to the practices and following their advice. May you achieve success in your efforts!

This booklet contains oral instructions given to Ven. Gelong Karma Jiga by Khenchen Tai Situ Rinpoche, Ven. Thrangu Rinpoche, Tenga Tulku, Yongjey Minjur Rinpoche, Chöje Akong Tulku Rinpoche, Ringu Tulku and the Ven. Lama Yeshe Losal Rinpoche over the last 30 years. Any mistakes are my own.

Sarva Mangalam, may goodness prevail.

The Venerable Gelong Karma Jiga with Choje Lama Akong Tulku Rinpoche the found-er of Samye Ling Monastery and The Venerable Lama Yeshe Losal Rinpoche, Abbot and Retreat Master of Samye Ling Monastery in Scotland.

The Venerable Gelong Karma Jiga as the Guest of Honour of the 18th Dulmo Choje
Rinpoche, the highest living Kagyu Lama in Tibet, during the yearly Guru Rinpoche
celebrations held at Damkar Monastery in Tibet in celebration of his attainment.

Karma Jiga with the 18th Dulmo Choje Rinpoche, Choje Lama Akong Tulku Rinpoche and the other esteemed Tulkus and guests on the final day of the Guru Rinpoche celebration at Damkar Monastery in Tibet.

The 18th Dulmo Choje Rinpoche, the highest living Kagyu Lama in Tibet, presenting the Venerable Gelong Karma Jiga with a silver and gold Guru Rinpoche Statue after the yearly Guru Rinpoche celebrations held at Damkar Monastery in Tibet, where he was guest of honour.

7. Suggested Session Prayers

For buddhist practitioners all these prayers have value and meaning.
The prayers are in Tibetan phonetics. You can choose to recite either both
Tibetan and English or for those who are not Buddhist just English will do.
It is the meaning that's important.

Prayer To The Root Teacher

Pal-den tsa-way la-ma rin-po chay
da gee chay or pen day den shook Ia
ka trin chen peu go nay jay soong tay
koo soong tuk chay ngeu drup tsal doo sol.(once)

Glorious, Precious Root-Guru,
Who sits on a lotus and moon seat above my head,
I pray, that in your great kindness, you take me into your care
And grant me the Siddhis of Body, Speech and Mind

Refuge Prayer

Sawnjay cheu tang tsok chee chok nam Ia,
chang choop bar doo da nee chap soom chee,
dak gee jin so jee pay sonam jee
dro Ia pen jeer sawnjay droop par sho (3 times)

Until I become enlightened,
I take refuge in the Buddha, Dharma and Sangha,
I dedicate any virtue accumulated through this practice,
to benefit all beings in order that they too may become Buddha

31

8. Increasing the positive

If you are not a Buddhist Practitioner you may find it beneficial to recite
The Four Limitless Contemplations followed by the
Dedication prayer to end the session.
This will increase the efficacy of your practice and benefit others.

The Four Limitless Contemplations

Semchen tamche day wa dang, day way ju tang den par jur chik,
doo-ngal dang ,doo-ngal jee, jutang tralwar jur-chik
du-ngal may pay day wa dampa-dang, mindral war jur-chik
nyay-ring, cha dang, dang dral way, tang-nyom, chempola naypar jur-chik. (3 times)

May all beings have happiness and the causes of happiness.
May they all be free from suffering and the causes of suffering
May they never be deprived of true happiness, devoid of any suffering.
May they abide in great impartiality,
free from attachment to loved ones and aversion to others

Dedication Of Merit

Sonam di yi tamche zik pan yi
Top nay nyay pay dra nam pam chay nay
Je-gar nak chee ba lap druk pa yee
See pay tso lay dro war drol war sho.

Through the virtue of this practice, may all the mental impurity be
overcome and may all beings be liberated from the ocean of samsara,
stirred by the waves of birth, old age, sickness and death.